GOD'S LOVE

GOD'S LOVE

Inspirational Poems and Life Stories

Dear Pastor Preston & Jean —
a simple token of
our christian fellowship

Linda C. Masibay
2-28-09

Linda C. Masibay

To order additional copies of this book, contact:
Xlibris Corporation
1-888-795-4274
www.Xlibris.com
Orders@Xlibris.com
39155

CONTENTS

DEDICATION

In memory of my beloved parents Pacifico L. Masibay and
Consuelo L. Cabansag; of my brothers Dillo and Rudy; of my
sister-in-law Nenita E. Masibay, my brother-in-law Virgilio
Bernardo, my nephew Genaro M. de Guzman,
my niece Abigail E. Masibay. In honor of my siblings
and in-laws Artemio and Adela Masibay; Jose and
Felicidad Masibay; Consolacion M. and Hector De Guzman;
Orlando C. Masibay, Iluminada M. Bernardo,
and Angelito P. Masibay, who in one way or
another have inspired me to write these poems.

Acknowledgement

My special thanks and appreciation to my Church Family, the Northern Illinois Conference of the United Methodist Church, which became my inspiration with my first poem "GOD'S LOVE", when I worked for the Conference as Program Staff in 1977, to the members of Cosmopolitan United Church in Melrose Park, Illinois, and to the San Vicente United Methodist Church, Inc. members, Zaragoza, Nueva Ecija, Philippines. In gratitude and sincere thanks to my blood family, the Masibays and the Cabansags, siblings, in-laws, nieces, nephews, who have been so patient encouraging me to pursue my passion for poetry as they read and share their thoughts at every poem I write. In recognition of my friends and associates, members of the Mekong Circle International especially Ken & Minerva Will who even gave me a chrome emblem 'PEACE" in response to my poem "Let There Be Peace" and my personal Crusade for Peace letter. To the late Cynthia Chow, owner of the Dietary Consulting group I work for who made an interesting comment, "I didn't know you have other talent Linda, you should pursue it," as she read my poem John F. Kennedy Jr. The members of my team trained on Humans Being More by Nikken, Inc., who have given their great comments and critiques to encourage me to keep on writing poems. In loving memory of my beloved parents Pacifico L. Masibay and Consuelo L. Cabansag, who had been my partners in my faith journey from early childhood days to their last breath of life and love. For without these loved ones this inspirational Book of Poems would not be in your homes as a published book to share the talent and gifts God has given me.

My first poem "God's Love" became the result of my inspirational experiences working with ordained and non-ordained servants in God's vineyard as a Program Staff. As I was leaving the Conference job I suddenly thought of writing a poem. I was so thrilled when I received a letter from the International Library of Poetry / poetry.com informing me that my poem had been selected to be published in the Edition they were working on at the time! As I received my copy of the book where my first poem was published, I was so inspired I decided to continue with my passion for poetry!

My personal experience in writing is that, no matter what I have as a title or an idea to put down in writing as a poem, if the Holy Spirit doesn't nudge me, nothing comes out in my mind to merit writing a poem.

GOD'S LOVE

BEYOND ALL BARRIERS GOD'S LOVE PREVAILS,
BEYOND ALL DIFFERENCES GOD'S LOVE EXISTS;
BEYOND ALL DIFFICULTIES GOD'S LOVE OVERCOMES,
BEYOND ALL CONFLICTS GOD'S LOVE SURROUNDS.

WE'VE GOT THE PEACE THAT PASSETH UNDERSTANDING,
WE'VE GOT THE GREATEST LOVE A PERSON CAN HAVE,
THE LOVE THAT GIVES UP OWN LIFE FOR FRIENDS.

PASS IT ON FOR LIFE IS BUT SHORT,
HOARD IT NOT SO MANY ARE THIRSTY;
KEEP IT IN CIRCULATION
FOR, IN THE FINAL HOUR
THE RECIPIENT WILL BE YOU AND ME.

My second poem "LITTLE ANGELS" was written as a personal reaction to a Mother in my home state of Illinois who drowned her three children. Yet her loving husband had so much love and understanding he would not lay blame on his wife, rather he did forgive her and had such compassion for her after the ordeal!

LITTLE ANGELS

LITTLE ANGELS, CHILDREN OF JOY,
GIFTS OF LOVE YOU SHOWERED US,
CHEERFUL TWINKLES IN YOUR LOVELY EYES
HOW WILL I NOT REMEMBER ALWAYS?

MOMENTS OF LAUGHTER WE SHARED TOGETHER,
TOUCH OF GENTLENESS IN SUCH INNOCENT LIVES
I WILL TREASURE YOUR MEMORY FOREVER.

YOU GAVE NEW MEANING TO LIFE AS A CHILD.
INSPIRATION YOU WERE, YOU ARE, AND ALWAYS WILL BE.
AS I CHERISH WHAT'S LEFT OF THE HUGS AND KISSES
WHEN WE CELEBRATE, RECOGNIZE,
AND APPRECIATE EACH OTHER.

GOD GRANTS US PEACE, COMFORT AND JOY,
WHEREVER YOU ARE NOW, WHEREVER I AM.
LITTLE ANGELS, CHILDREN OF GOD,
APPLES OF MY EYES, I LOVE YOU ALL.

The third poem "VICTORY OVER DEFEAT", a very timely poem inspired by the simultaneous deaths of two internationally loved women the same year. These women are no other than the Beloved Mother Teresa, an Albanian, but established her famous charity/orphanage in India for the . . . "poorest among the poor . . ."; and Her Royal Highness (HRH) Princess Diana of the United Kingdom. Their undying love for people especially the downtrodden . . . 'poorest among the poor", and those who are infected with HIV/AIDS made me realize that these two modern women heroes have not died in vain but rather both conquered defeat by the victories of their deeds! This realization was inspired by the Holy Spirit.

VICTORY OVER DEFEAT

I LIVE BECAUSE I LOVE.
I LOVE BECAUSE I CARE.
I CARE BECAUSE I LIVE.

BECAUSE I LIVE I EXPERIENCE FAILURES.
BECAUSE I LOVE I EXPERIENCE HURTS.
BECAUSE I CARE I HAVE DISSAPPOINTMENTS
AND FRUSTRATIONS.

BUT, FAILURES, DISAPPOINTMENTS AND FRUSTRATIONS
ARE ALL FIBERS OF STRENGTH
WOVEN INTO FAITH THAT ENDURES;
WOVEN INTO GOD'S LOVE
THAT GIVES US VICTORY OVER DEFEAT.

My next poem: "FAITH" was scribbled on a piece of paper while I was looking out on an airline window gazing over the snow-white fluffy beds of clouds beneath the plane as it soared above those clouds! Flying in such a huge metal bird (I call the airplane as such) looking at all the passengers aboard, and the airline crew, I felt the Holy Spirit nudging me to write something about my own Faith journey.

FAITH

WHEN I AM DOWN AND WEARY,
HURTING TO MY SOUL AND DREARY
I SEARCH THE WORLD
FOR COMFORT AND PEACE.

I LOOK TO PEOPLES' FACES, I SEE A SMILE.
I AM ENCOURAGED TO KEEP ON GOING.
I SEE A GLOOMY FACE
A CHEERFUL VOICE SAYS
I'LL LIFT THAT FACE IN PRAYER.
I SEE PAIN IN SOMEONE'S FACE
I HEAR A WHISPER
I'LL HEAL THE PAIN YOU SUFFER.

I LOOK TO NATURE AND MARVEL AT CREATION
I SEE A HEAVY CAST, RAIN IS COMING
TO SOAK AND DRENCH THE EARTH THAT'S DRY.
I SEE THE SUNSHINE BRIGHT AND FRIENDLY,
SOMEONE'S HAPPY, DANCING IN CREATION.
I HEAR THE VOICE OF THUNDER LOUD AS IT SOUNDS
A VOICE CAUTIONS ME "BE NOT AFRAID,
A RAINBOW IS IN SIGHT AS MY COVENANT WITH YOU."

As a Dietitian Nutritionist my favorite walk for cause is "Walk for Hunger" (CROP WALK) sponsored by the Proviso Food Pantry in a near West Suburb of Illinois. Year after year my sister, my nephew and I would join our Cluster Churches to walk for hunger and solicit people to sponsor us so we can raise funds for the hungry around us. I appeal to my blood families, my Church Family / Community of Faith, friends and associates to sponsor us and make donations. We have a church member who loved to run instead of walking and he was our biggest fundraiser as he gathered the most donations for the church walk. It's a six-mile (10 Km) stretch of walk. After one of those walks I felt the nudge to write yet another poem. Thus my poem, "We Walk, We Run".

WE WALK WE RUN

FROM THE DARK GHETTOS AROUND THE GLOBE,
I CAN SEE SKIN AND BONES ROAMING THE STREETS.
THEIR DEEP-SET EYES PENETRATING MY SOUL SAYING
"YOU SAW ME HUNGRY BUT DIDN'T FEED ME"

THOSE WHO ARE TOUCHED TOOK TIME TO WALK.
TOOK TIME TO RUN, ASKED FAMILIES AND FRIENDS.
YES, IT ONLY TAKES AT LEAST AN HOUR TO RUN,
THREE HOURS TO WALK AND SHARE WHAT WE HAVE.
AT OUR DINNER TABLES WE HAVE CHOICES OF FOOD.
IT SINKS MY HEART IF FOOD GOES TO THE GARBAGE
IF DAY'S LEFT OVERS END UP IN THE DUMPSTER
BECAUSE IT DIDN'T APPEAL TO PEOPLES' TASTE BUDS!
A STILL SMALL VOICE KEEPS REMINDING ME,
THE REST OF THE WORLD HAVE NO CHOICE
BUT TO GO TO BED HUNGRY AT EACH CLOSING DAY!
A CHALLENGE TO US; WON'T WE KEEP THEM IN MIND?
THE SKIN AND BONES ROAMING THE EARTH.
NUTRITIOUS MEALS ALL GOD'S CHILDREN DESERVE
NOT ABUNDANCE ONLY OF THE WORLD'S AFFLUENT.

Since my childhood, Church has been a vital part of my being. I owe this passion from my beloved parents who had been my partners in our journey of faith together with my siblings. As I was growing up I used to go with my Father during my free times visiting farm tenants and their families. In those long treks Father would repeatedly share with me some thoughts on 'sharing'. He would state . . . "we are not rich, yet we are not that poor. But there are those less fortunate around us who need more than we do as they barely have anything. Therefore bear in mind to always share what you have if you see a need." The result of these inspirations is my poem "Born to Live and to Love".

BORN TO LIVE AND TO LOVE

BORN TO LIVE AMONG ALL OF CREATIONS.
LIFE WE RECEIVED FREELY WITH EMOTIONS,
AND SENSES TO SEE, THE BEAUTY OF THE EARTH.
TO SMELL THE FRAGRANCE IN THE AIR,
TO FEEL THE GENTLE BREEZE SWEEP MY HAIR.

SENSE OF TOUCH AS I MOVE AROUND
CARING FOR, SERVING OTHERS WITH LOVE ABOUND.
LIVING IS ALL LOVING, AND LOVING IS LIVING.
THE WORLD IS IN CHAOS WARS KEEP ON GOING.
ABANDONED CHILDREN FILL UP ORPHANAGES.
PARENTS AGING LONGING FOR WARM EMBRACES.

TEENAGERS AND YOUTH SEARCHING FOR IDENTITY
LOOKING FOR LIFE'S PURPOSE WITH QUALITY.
YOUNG ADULT SOARING LIKE EAGLES
FEELING NO SATISFACTION IN THEIR RESTLESSNESS.
THEY ARE THE REASONS I WAS BORN TO LIVE.
SOMEONE HAS TO CARE FOR AND LOVE TO THEM GIVE.

I attended a Nikken Incorporated two-day Humans Being More Training. Our team was composed of five members coming from different states around the nation. On the second day of training I brought with me my poems and gave them each a set of copies. One of them asked me to write a poem for him. He gave me the title he wants . . . "Un-prayed Answer". I asked him what was that un-prayed answer. And he said about us his co-team members, that, somehow, we seemed to be an answer to a current need we weren't even aware of. It turned out he was inspired by our team's compassion and love for each other as we went through the two-day tough training.

UNPRAYED ANSWER

THE BEAUTY OF GOD'S MYSTERIOUS WAYS,
ON BENDED KNEES I PRAY MY BURDEN TO HIM LAY.
HE ANSWERS MY PLEAS, ASSURANCE I FEEL.
WHAT HE KNOWS I NEED HE FULFILLS.

TAKEN BY SURPRISE ONE DAY,
BLESSINGS I RECEIVED, I DIDN'T EVEN PRAY.
NEW FRIENDS I MET SHOWERED ME WITH LOVE,
NEVER I EXPECTED GIFTS FROM ABOVE.

CARING, LOVING, THOUGHTFUL NEW FRIENDS
WHO ENCOURAGED ME AND GAVE ME HOPE
TO PICK UP THE PIECES, GO FOR THE TRENDS.
I NOW CAN MOVE ON WITH TOOLS I HAVE TO COPE.

AS I LOOKED AROUND, I SEE BOUNTIFUL BLESSINGS
I TAKE FOR GRANTED AS EACH DAY I LIVE.
THESE ARE OTHER ANSWERS FOR HELPINGS
UNPRAYED FOR, YET OUR LOVING GOD TO US GIVES.

July 4, 2006 was fast approaching and again I felt a nudge to write one more poem. And I thought what title would I give to this poem? As I watched TV newscast everyday, violence of war and other atrocities occupied most of the news as the United States is in its third year of the war in Iraq. Our uniformed troops mostly in their prime of youth were being killed innocently as violence spread around the world, mostly in the Middle East. I thought I might as well give this poem the title of "Let Freedom Ring".

LET FREEDOM RING

FROM EAST TO WEST, AND NORTH TO SOUTH
AROUND THE WORLD AT PLANET EARTH
THE SOUND OF GUNS AND BOMBS PREVAIL.
SITTING SILENT IN THE U.S.A. THE LIBERTY BELL.
COULD IT BE LET LOOSE TO ONCE AGAIN
RING WITH LIBERTY THE FREEDOM RING?

DISABLED AMERICAN VETERANS' MESSAGE:
"FREEDOM ISN'T FREE" INDEED IT ISN'T!
FOR EVERY WAR PRECIOUS LIVES WE LOST,
HEALTHY BODIES AND HEALTHY MINDS OF YOUTH
COME BACK HOME WITH SHATTERED THOUGHTS
FAMILIES BROKEN, WHAT PRICE WE PAY!

GLOBAL-WISE WE'RE ALL ONE FAMILY
OF HUMANS BEING MORE, LET'S LIVE IT TRULY!
PEACEFUL CO-EXISTENCE, INTERDEPENDENCE,
KEYWORDS TO LIVE IN PEACE, NOT INDEPENDENCE!
ERE WE COMPETE TO BE ON TOP AT OTHER'S EXPENSE.
LET FREEDOM RING WITH SWEET MELODY
FROM THE HEARTS AND SOULS, LET FREEDOM RING!
TOMORROW'S LEADERS YOUTH OF TODAY
LET FREEDOM RING FOR GENERATIONS YET TO SING!

As I continue my Faith Journey I would be in continuous search for the Holy Spirit to inspire me to write poems. I have to recall the Christmas season is just around the corner with the Season's message of Peace. I thought it is but fitting and proper to honor this special season with a poem that sends the message of Peace to everyone.

LET THERE BE PEACE

THE FRAGRANCE OF SPRING IS IN THE AIR
THE DEW DROPS ARE SPARKLING AND DANCING.
THE WIND BLOWS THE LEAVES.
CUDDLING IN ITS CARE THE GRASS.
NATURE HAS IT SO THE PLANET EARTH
IS FLOODED WITH BEAUTY.
PARADISE REGAINED AS I GAZED
LOOKING AT THE HORIZON IN BOUNTY.

WHAT A GLORIOUS WORLD
THE CREATOR HANDED TO US.
SO WE MAY ALL LIVE IN PEACE AND HARMONY,
WITH LOVE AND CARE FOR EACH OTHER AS HUMANS.
TAKE A MOMENT TO THINK AND PONDER
HOW MAY WE PROMOTE PEACEFUL CO-EXISTENCE
AMIDST OUR DIVERSITY AND DIFFERENCES.
YES, LET THERE BE PEACE AND
LET IT BEGIN WITH ME TO ALL IN THE UNIVERSE!

I was listening to one of my favorite radio stations, FM 90.1, while driving one day and a lady's voice was narrating an essay she wrote about her uniformed husband currently in Iraq. It was about her belief that someday her uniformed spouse will soon come home. Suddenly, I felt the Holy Spirit nudge me to write another poem with the title in mind "I Believe". So the next poem is just that "I Believe".

I BELIEVE

I BELIEVE FOR EVERY BREATH OF AIR WE BREATHE
GOD'S BREATH OF LOVE IS THERE.
BUT IN THE BUSYNESS OF THE WORLD WE LIVE IN,
GOD'S LOVE SEEMS SO FAR OUT OF REACH.
I BELIEVE IN GOD'S LOVE FOR ALL HUMAN FAMILIES,
HE GAVE US HIS SON TO BE OUR SAVIOR.

I BELIEVE THE PRINCE OF PEACE PROCLAIMED
"PEACE ON EARTH GOODWILL TOWARD MEN"
WILL SOMEDAY GRANT PEACE THAT PASSETH
UNDERSTANDING AMIDST THE CHAOS IN OUR PATHS.
I BELIEVE AND TRUST THE HUMAN IN US
WILL COME TO GRASP GOD'S LOVE AND PEACE.

I BELIEVE IN THE RAINBOW COVENANT
THAT NEVER AGAIN NOAH'S ARK STORY
BE REPEATED BUT RATHER BE REFRESHED
THAT HUMANKIND WILL NOT VANISH
FROM THE FACE OF THE EARTH INSTEAD
WILL COME JUBILANT FOR THE GOD OF LOVE.

While watching a Christmas video, featuring the meaning of Christmas the drummer boy began marching beating his drum, and singing 'Pum rum pu pum pum". The rest of the world watched him pass by, until he came to the manger, cheerfully greeted Mary, Joseph and the Baby Jesus, offered nothing but himself, his drum and his song! What a powerful scene for me! I was inspired, took a pen and a piece of paper to write "The Drummerboy".

THE DRUMMERBOY

MY EYES WELLED WITH TEARS
AS THE DRUMMERBOY
MARCHED WITHOUT FEARS.
MOVE FORWARDTHE HOLY SCENE WITH JOY.
OFFERED HIMSELF, HIS DRUM, HIS SONG.
ALL THAT HE HAS,
TO THE CHILD WE'VE WAITED LONG.

SUDDENLY IT DAWNED ON ME
GOD GAVE THIS GIFT THAT ALL MAY BELIEVE.
CHRIST CAME FOR ALL, FIRST THE WORD,
THEN THE FLESH DWELT AMONGST THE WORLD.
BUT MOST, FOR THE DRUMMERBOY IN US!

I was at a Church Service on a Thanksgiving Day. As I listened to the Thanksgiving story the Preacher narrated, my thoughts started weaving words for a thanksgiving poem "Thank you God"

THANK YOU GOD

FOR THE UNIVERSE YOU'VE CREATED,
WE THANK YOU GOD!
FOR EVERY CREATURE YOU ENTRUSTED TO US,
WE GIVE THEE THANKS!
LIGHT, AT DAY TIME, FOR US TO TOIL AND LIVE.
DARK, AND QUIET AT NIGHT TIME, FOR US TO REST.

FOR ALL OF YOUR CREATION WE ARE GRATEFUL!
FOR THE LIFE YOU GAVE THAT WE MAY FULLY LIVE
GIVER OF LIFE WE THANK YOU!

GREAT AWESOME GOD WE OWE YOU EVERYTHING!
GRANT US WISDOM TO BE WISE,
STRENGTHEN OUR FAITH AS WE TRUST YOU!
LOVE AND COMPASSION WE ASK OF THEE,
THAT WE MAY SHARE THESE, YOUR GIFTS.

FORGIVENESS IS THERE FOR OUR ASKING
AS WE FORGIVE OTHERS, WHO DO US WRONG.
FOR ALL OUR NEEDS YOU DO PROVIDE.
OBEDIENCE TO YOUR WILL YOU ASK OF US
HELP US YOUR CHILDREN TO BE FAITHFUL,
TO BE GRATEFUL, AND TO BE THANKFUL ALWAYS!

One day I was feeling alone in my dining room. I tried to perk up but only to be back in the valley of loneliness. I started thinking of my families, friends, far and beyond my immediate touch. Then thoughts came flowing in my mind. I started to jot them down, and without realizing it I've written a poem, "The Greatest of All Hope".

THE GREATEST OF ALL HOPE

FROM THE DEPTHS OF TRAGEDY AND DEPRESSION,
WHO CAN I TURN TO?
FROM THE NICHES OF NEEDS AND CRACKS OF
DISAPPOINTMENTS, WHO SHOULD I GO TO?

FRIENDS AND COMRADES LOST IN THE BUSYNESS OF
THE WORLD. WOULD YOU SPARE TIME WHEN I
NEED YOU? YES, THE COMMUNITY OF FAITH, OF
FRIENDS, ARE WILLING TO RESPOND. BLOOD FAMILIES
TOGETHER YOU STAND BEHIND ME. GIVING SUPPORT
TO KEEP ME UP AND SUSTAIN MY FAITH.
THANK YOU ALL FOR SUCH BLESSINGS IN MY LIFE!

IN MY SOLITUDE I REMEMBER THE SCRIPTURES SAY
AGAIN AND AGAIN . . . "I AM WITH YOU ALWAYS EVEN
UNTO THE ENDS OF THE EARTH" . . . YES INDEED, MY
GREATEST FRIEND AND HOPE. JESUS HAS ALWAYS
BEEN WHEREVER I WAS, I AM, AND I WILL BE!
NEVER HAS FORGOTTEN ME, NEVER ABANDONED ME.
THANK YOU JESUS YOU ARE SUCH A GREAT FRIEND!
THE SWEET SMELL OF SPRING BROUGHT BY THE
COOL SHOWERS OF RAIN.
TINY FLOWERS IN ARRAY OF COLORS,
GREEN LITTLE LEAVES AND BALLS OF BUDS
TOGETHER LAUGHING TO GREET SPRING.
GIVING HOPE PAST THE GLOOM OF WINTER,
PAST, PRESENT AND FUTURE WINTERS OF LIFE.

AND YES, THE BEAUTIFUL LILIES DANCING TO THE
GLOW OF SUNSHINE TO USHER THE GREATEST OF ALL
HOPE . . . EASTER . . . RESURRECTION, THE FINAL VICTORY!

As I reflect on peoples' dreams and mine there seems a common wish, that of becoming a success, in finances, in career, in fame, in totality, gain acceptance by our peers. Then I began to reminisce my own life and that of loved ones around me. I kept going back to my Father's legacy of sharing, thus this poem "Success".

SUCCESS

OH THE SWEET TASTE OF SUCCESS ALL DREAM OF.
IF ONLY I CAN BE A SUCCESS WHEREOF,
I'LL DO ALL I CAN TO BE IN THAT HIGH LOFT.

SILENCE, AN INNERVOICE INTERRUPTED MY DREAM.
WHERE IS THIS VOICE FLASHING LIKE A BEAM?

SUCCESS, YOU WANT TO BE, WILLING TO DO ALL.
THE VOICE HAD SPOKEN, RESPONDED TO MY CALL.
HOW ARE YOU WILLING TO GIVE UP FOR OTHERS?

NOTHING FOR OTHERS BUT ALL FOR MYSELF,
POSSESS POWER, BE IN STARDOM, MATERIAL WEALTH.
ALL TO HAVE, FOR HUMANS IS SUCCESS.

I AM WHO I AM, FOR YOU I GAVE MY LIFE.
I SERVED THOSE IN NEED, HEALED THOSE IN PAIN.
WITH WORDS, THOUGHTS, PRAYERS AND DEEDS.
WAKE UP WHILE THERE IS YET FLICKER OF LIGHT.
DO WHAT I DID, FOR, A CROWN OF SUCCESS
AWAITS YOU WHEN THE TIME IS RIGHT.

Worldwide the name Kennedy is known for different reasons. But when the plane John F. Kennedy, Jr. was piloting plunged into the vast water never to rise again in flesh, the world was in shock. I have a friend whose profession as a Chef in the restaurant where John F. Kennedy, Jr. usually ate a late dinner, enabled her to meet him. He normally ate alone every evening by 10:00o'clock. Oh how she wept and grieved because at the time of the tragedy she was out of the country attending a convention! I thought of reflecting on John's stardom, ending with this poem, "John F. Kennedy, Jr.".

JOHN F. KENNEDY, Jr.

LIFE HE LEARNED TO LOVE,
FOR THE OPPORTUNITIES IT OFFERED.
TO SHARE THE BLESSINGS HE RECEIVED
FROM THE ALMIGHTY GOD!
TO ENJOY ADVENTURES, EVEN AS HE CONQUERED
THE VAST SPACE WITH THE GIANT METAL BIRD
LIFE, THE MYSTERIES OF WHICH NO ONE FULLY
UNDERSTANDS.
HE HAS SEARCHED AND SEARCHED FOR HIS PLACE IN
THE SUN.

FOUND IT ONE MIGHT THINK, SUCCESS AND FAME
THE LEGACIES HIS PARENTS HAD GIVEN HIS NAME
ONLY TO FEEL CRAVING FOR MORE THAN NAME AND FAME.

FREEDOM, FREEDOM TO BE HIM HE HAD WANTED
A SIMPLE ONE LIKE US IN HIMSELF BELOVED.
PLANNED TO LIVE LONGER WITH HIS LOVELY WIFE
DREAMED A LONGER JOURNEY TO SAVOR THE
FULLNESS OF LIFE.
FLYING HE TREASURED AS HE SOARED TO THE SKY
EXPERIENCING EXCITEMENT,
BEING HAPPY ABOVE SO HIGH.
HERE HE IS IN THE PEAK OF LIFE, BUT HE HAS TO LEAVE.
HIS LOVE FOR LIFE HE PASSES ON TO US, PASS IT ON.
REMEMBER HIM, WE WILL, AS HEAVEN HIM RECEIVED.

The well known natural calamity "Tsunami" that had happened touched my heart with such sadness and so with mixed feelings of what to do and how to deal with such natural disaster I felt a nudge to write a poem: "Away from the Manger" since it was about the season of Thanksgiving and Christmas when it happened.

AWAY FROM THE MANGER

AWAY FROM THE MANGER CHRISTMAS IS LOST
CHRISTMAS BECOMES A HOLIDAY SHOPPING FROST.
INDEED IT GOES AWASH TO THE FAR BEACHES
THE SINGING OF THE ANGELS DROWNED BY SLEEZE
OF EARTHLY PLEASURES CALLING FROM AFAR.

DAY AFTER THANKSGIVING STARTS THE holy CALL
COME TO THE SHORELINE OF MY GREAT GIFTS
FOR EACH AND EVERY LOVE ONE IN YOUR LISTS.
AS THE COLD WINTER SEASON RINGS
THE JOYFUL LURES OF VACATION BEGINS.
COME TO THE BEAUTY AND WARMTH OF NATURE
IN THESE BLESSED PARTS OF THE UNIVERSE.
WITH ALL THESE TEMPTATIONS THE TRUE MEANING
OF THE FIRST CHRISTMAS CERTAINLY ENGULFED,
IF NOT FORGOTTEN, MISSED AND IGNORED.
THE MIRACLE OF A DISASTER IN ITS URGENCY BRINGS
INNER GOODNESS OUT OF US AND WE BECOME
A FAMILY UNITED LEAVING BEHIND MISGIVINGS.

I have a high school classmate whose birthday falls during the advent season and as I thought of us celebrating her birthday during our younger years I had to think of some kind of remembering her that I could relate every time the advent season begins. After one of those celebrations, I came back home and was inspired to write a poem. "Happy Birthday".

HAPPY BIRTHDAY

REMEMBER ADVENT THE WAITING FOR CHRISTMAS,
ANTICIPATING THE BIRTH OF THE LORD, JESUS CHRIST.
THE WOMB OF YOUR MOTHER AN ADVENT OF A MASS
SHE CARRIED FOR LONG, CARED AND LOVED TO LAST.

TO GIVE BIRTH TO THIS BABY SHE HAD WAITED FOR.
YOUR CHRISTMAS IS THE DAY WHEN YOU WERE BORN.
CELEBRATE LIFE, GIVE THANKS FOR GLORIOUS MORN.

REJOICE IN THE LORD, REJOICE WITH FAMILIES.
REMINISCE OF BYGONE DAYS, UNTIL THIS DAY
THE PRESENT, THE BIG DAY, YOUR BIRTHDAY!

THEN, IN THE YEARS AHEAD DO LOOK FORWARD.
FOCUS WHERE YOU WANT TO BE, MARCH ONWARD,
BEARING THE CHRISTIAN FAITH YOU EMBRACED
AND . . . 'LET YOUR LIGHT SO SHINE BEFORE ALL
THAT THEY MAY SEE YOUR GOOD WORKS AND
GIVE GLORY TO YOUR GOD IN HEAVEN!

In this century of modern medical technologies, advancements in medical sciences indeed result in amazing discoveries of drugs and medicines that offers relief to almost majority of human illnesses. Yet, the power of God's healing mercies should not be ignored. The holistic approach to medical nutrition therapy is getting grounds. Thus, this poem "Healing Comes to Us" I wrote.

HEALING COMES TO US

THE POWER OF HEALING IS IN GOD'S HANDS
AS PARTNERS WE FOLLOW GOD'S COMMANDS.
THRU JESUS CHRIST THE GREAT PHYSICIAN
HEALING WILL COME TO US WITH HIS LOVE.
AS HEALING COMES TO ALL WHO BELIEVED
WE WILL BE HEALED IF HIM WE RECEIVE.

STRENGTH AND ENDURANCE THESE WE NEED.
IN TIMES OF SICKNESS AND PAIN, AS WE HEED
TO THE GREAT PHYSICIAN'S WILL AND WAY.
OUR FAITHFUL PRAYERS DAY BY DAY
WE OFFER TO GOD AS WE RISE AND SHINE.

As mentioned earlier I work for a Dietary Consulting Group based in Chicago, Illinois. This consulting firm is owned by the late Cynthia Chow, who made a comment she didn't know I have another talent, that of writing poems. She even teased me why not pursue this talent and become a poet and author. Now that I have the opportunity to compile my poems into a book of poems and as I planned for my retirement in May 2008 I thought it is but fitting and proper to write a poem in honor of Cynthia Chow.

CYNTHIA CHOW

C—ARING AND COMPASSIONATE SHE HAS ALWAYS BEEN,
Y—OUTHFUL VIBRANCE INFECTIOUS AND CONTAGIOUS,
N—EVER DID SHE HOARD FROM ANYONE SHE ENCOUNTERS.
T—RUTH AND HONESTY SHE EXEMPLIFIES TO ALL.
H—EALING AND LOVE WHEN GOING GETS ROUGH,
I—NDEED SHE OFFERS WHEN SOMEONE IS DOWN.
A—LL THESE SHE HAD BEEN IN THE FULLNESS OF HER LIFE.
C—OULD SOMEONE NOT REMEMBER,
H—OW WONDERFUL AND LOVING A PERSON SHE IS?
O—N THE PEAK OF HER LIFE WE LOST HER
W—HY, IS THE QUESTION ONLY GOD CAN ANSWER.

We are all familiar with the Christmas song "The Twelve Days of Christmas". However, I thought, why not have a real Christmas—focused life stories, observations, and experiences of the same title? So, reminiscing Biblical scriptures related to advent season I gathered the following scriptures and thought of real life stories, observations, and experiences to reflect these scriptures for Advent.

I share these life stories, observations, and experiences, though these happened on different times during my journey, not necessarily on the Twelve Days of Christmas. I reflect every Christmas Day I have had these opportunities in life of sharing, giving, caring and sacrificing for others. That, Christmas is not just once a year on Christmas Day celebration and gift-giving but is an all-year sharing of love and compassion to those in need around us!

We do not need to wait for Christmas Day to do something good, share and give gifts of love and compassion to others. Every minute is an opportunity for us if we look around and are willing to celebrate the meaning of Christmas in our lives! We do say. "It is better to give than to receive." Let us then put some actions into these words. Our daily armor to carry with us is 1 Corinthians 13:13 "There are three things that remain—Faith, Hope, and Love—and the greatest of these is Love."

Matthew 7:12—"Do for others what you want them to do for you. This is the teaching of the laws of Moses in a nutshell."

ON THE FIRST DAY OF CHRISTMAS

A YOUNG HIGH SCHOOL STUDENT RAN AWAY FROM HOME,
WANDERED FROM PLACE TO PLACE. AND WOUND UP
IN THE MASIBAY HOME IN THE PHILIPPINES.
HE LIVED WITH US TO BECOME PART OF OUR FAMILY.

WE HELPED HIM THROUGH HIGH SCHOOL,
TO THE PRESTIGIOUS UNIVERSITY OF THE PHILIPPINES,
TO EARN HIS B.S. DEGREE, HIS GRADUATE DEGREE
AND TO HIS UTMOST GOAL, A Ph. D.

TWO DECADES LATER WHEN MY FATHER DIED
HE AND HIS WIFE CAME TO JOIN OUR FAMILY REUNION.
IN HIS FAMILY MEMBER SHARING HE OFFERED HIS Ph. D.
EDUCATION ACHIEVEMENT IN MEMORY OF MY FATHER
AND THANKED THE REST OF US SIBLINGS
IN GIVING HIM THE OPPORTUNITY OF A NEW LIFE.

Matthew 15:32—" . . . I have compassion on the multitude, because they continue with me now three days and have nothing to eat: and I will not send them away fasting, lest they faint in the way."

ON THE SECOND DAY OF CHRISTMAS

IN THE 70'S A STRONG STORM HITS THE PHILIPPINES
RESULTING IN FLOODED ROADS
AND HIGHWAYS, MOTORISTS STRANDED.
COUPLE OF UNITED METHODIST CLERGY
DROVE UP TO THE MASIBAY
FRONTYARD APPARENTLY STRANDED ASKED
MY FATHER IF THEY COULD
STAY IN FOR THE NIGHT WITH OUR FAMILY.
WELCOMED THEY WERE AND SO STAYED OVERNIGHT,
WERE PROVIDED SHELTER AND MEALS AS THEY SETTLED.
THE FLOOD HAS SUBSIDED AND HOMEWARD
BOUND THEY GOT BACK TO THEIR CAR
THANKFUL FOR SUCH A BLESSING OF A
FAMILY WHO TOOK THEM IN
WITH LOVE AND COMPASSION.

Isaiah 58:7—"I want you to share your food with the hungry and bring right into your own homes those who are helpless, poor and destitute. Clothe those who are cold."

ON THE THIRD DAY OF CHRISTMAS

AT SAYABOURY HOSPITAL, LAOS
WE JUST FINISHED OUR DINNER MEAL.
OUR MEDICAL DIRECTOR ANNOUNCED
"WE HAVE A YOUNG LAO GIRL
IN OUR O.P.D. ALL ALONE, NO PLACE TO STAY
FOR THE NIGHT"
OUR MEDICAL STAFF WENT SILENT,
EVERYONE LOOKING AT EACH
OTHER IN SILENCE. I COULD NOT STAND THE SILENCE
OPENED MY BIG MOUTH AND SAID, "DOC, I WILL
TAKE HER IN MY ROOM WITH ME."
THE GIRL WAS BROUGHT IN, I GAVE HER A NICE WARM BATH.
I RUMMAGED THROUGH OUR 'SOCIAL SERVICE BOX'
TO FIND CLOTHES TO WEAR. WE SHARED MY TWIN BED.
AS SHE LAY DOWN SHE LOOKED AT ME AND SAID
"KOP CHAI LAI LAI" (THANK YOU VERY MUCH).

I John 3:18—"My little children, let us not love in word, neither in tongue; but in deed and in truth."

ON THE FOURTH DAY OF CHRISTMAS

AT THE SAME SAYABOURY HOSPITAL
HAVING LUNCH WITH THE REST OF THE MEDICAL STAFF.
A NURSE CAME RUNNING AND SAID . . .
"WE NEED TYPE A / B BLOOD
TRANSFUSION IN THE OPERATING ROOM."
AGAIN THERE WAS SILENCE AROUND THE TABLE.
I STOOD UP, ASKED FOR A DRIVER. WE DROVE DOWN THE ROAD
TO THE C.M.A. HOME WHERE MISSIONARIES DON AND
SALLY DURLING WERE ALSO HAVING LUNCH.
I BEGGED WHO'S GOT A TYPE A/B BLOOD.
IN QUICK RESPONSE PASTOR DON GOT UP,
LEFT THEIR LUNCH TABLE AND CAME WITH US
TO THE HOSPITAL O.R. HE DONATED BLOOD
AS NEEDED AFTER WHICH HE SAID . . . "THANK YOU
FOR THE OPPORTUNITY AND GOD BLESS YOU.

2 Peter 1:6-8 "Next, learn to put aside your own desires so that you will become patient and godly, gladly letting God have His way with you. This will make possible the next step, which is for you to enjoy people and to like them. And finally you will grow to love them deeply. The more you go on in this way, the more you grow strong spiritually and become fruitful and useful to our Lord Jesus Christ."

ON THE FIFTH DAY OF CHRISTMAS

I WAS AT PAKSONG HOSPITAL, LAOS
DR. ALEX APPROACHED ME AND ASKED IF
I COULD HELP HIM WITH A PATIENT
WHO HAD BEEN COMATOSE FOR MONTHS.
I KNOW WHAT DR. ALEX WAS ASKING FOR.
A NUTRITIONAL INTERVENTION.

I ACCEPTED THE CHALLENGE AND TOGETHER
WE DREW A 24-HOUR SPECIALLY FORMULATED
TUBE FEEDING SUPPLEMENT VIA BIG SYRINGE
(A 16TH CENTURY MEDICALLY BACKWARD KINGDOM OF LAOS)

JUST AS I WAS ABOUT TO BE ASSIGNED IN ANOTHER
YET PROVINCIAL HOSPITAL,
THE PATIENT SUDDENLY OPENED HER EYES,
MOVED HER FINGERS AND LOOKED UP!
TALKING ABOUT MIRCALES, DR. ALEX SAID . . .
'THANK YOU LINDA FOR SUCH PATIENCE YOU HAD
LOOKING AFTER THIS LADY ROUND THE CLOCK . . .
THIS IS REALLY A MIRACLE.'

Luke 6:37 "Judge not, and ye shall not be judged; condemn not, and ye shall not be condemned: forgive and ye shall be forgiven."

ON THE SIXTH DAY OF CHRISTMAS

I WAS IN THE SAME PAKSONG HOSPITAL, LAOS
OUR MEDICAL STAFF RECEIVED AN ALERT NOTE
FROM THE 'VIETCONGS'. (VIETNAMESE COMMUNIST)
THAT OUR COMMUNITY WILL BE ATTACKED THAT NIGHT
AS VIETCONGTROOPS WILL CROSS THE FAMOUS
'HO CHI MINH TRAIL'. SO WE EXPECTED ENCOUNTERS
AND CROSSFIRESBETWEEN THE VIETCONGS
AND THE ROYAL LAO ARMY.

ONE OF OUR LAO KITCHEN WORKER APPROACHED ME
AND SAID . . . 'MISS LINDA, IF THIS HAPPENS TONIGHT
ALLOW ME TO SWITCH CLOTHES WITH YOU
SO YOU MAY LAY IN ONE OF THE HOSPITAL BEDS.
THE VIETCONGS WILL THINK YOU ARE
A LAOTIAN PATIENT AND WILL LEAVE YOU ALONE.'

WHAT A RISK! I THOUGHT OF JESUS
LAYING HIS LIFE FOR ALL OF US!
THEN, I THOUGHT AGAIN, THIS PERSON IS A BUDDHIST
BY RELIGION AND IS WILLING TO DO THIS FOR ME
A CHRISTIAN BY BIRTH? I WAS AWED AND SAID TO HIM
. . . 'OH MY GOD! THANK YOU! WE'LL BE OKAY TONIGHT'. . .
AND WE DID, NO ONE WAS HURT NOR INJURED
IN THE CROSSFIRES, THANKS GOD INDEED!

James 2:1 "Dear brothers, how can you claim that you belong to the Lord Jesus Christ, the Lord of glory, if you show favoritism to rich people and look down on poor people?"

ON THE SEVENTH DAY OF CHRISTMAS

I WAS RIDING IN A BUS HERE IN CHICAGO, IL, U.S.A.
THERE WAS THIS COO-COO LOOKING PERSON ASKING
EVERY PASSENGER FOR MONEY FOR HIS BUS FARE.
THANK GOD THERE WAS A KINDHEARTED
PASSENGER WHO COUNTED COINS
ENOUGH FOR THE COO-COO LOOKING
PERSON'S BUS FARE AND GAVE TO HIM.
THE COO-COO LOOKING PERSON
SMILED AND SAID . . . 'GOD BLESS YOU!'

James 2:14 "Dear brothers what's the use of saying that you have faith and are Christians if you aren't proving it by helping others? Will that kind of faith save anyone?"

ON THE EIGHT DAY OF CHRISTMAS

I RECEIVED A CALL FROM A HANDICAPPED
TRAINING WORKSHOP AT A SUBURBAN CHICAGO, IL ASKING
IF I WAS WILLING TO HIRE A HANDICAPPED FROM THEIR
TRAINING WORKSHOP. SHE SAID SHE WAS WILLING
TO COME AND HELP ME SUPERVISE THIS LADY,
ONE ON ONE. WITHOUT HESITATION I SAID 'YES'
SO WE ADDED THIS LADY TO OUR REGULAR STAFF.

HER PARENTS DROVE HER TO AND FROM WORK DAILY.
WHEN HER PARENTS SAW ME STILL AT WORK LATE EVENINGS,
THEY EXPRESSED APPRECIATION AND THANKS
FOR GIVING THEIR DAUGHTER AN OPPORTUNITY.
IN THOSE DAYS, FEW ESTABLISHMENTS
HIREDHANDICAPPED OR PEOPLE WITH DISABILITY.

ENCOURAGED BY THE PROGRESS OF THIS LADY,
I SUGGESTED TO HER PARENTS TO LOOK FOR
A FULL TIME AND MORE RESPONSIBLE TYPE OF JOB
AS I FELT THE LADY WAS READY TO MOVE UP.
THEY DID AND THEIR DAUGHTER
WAS BLESSED TO BE HIRED FULL TIME
AS WELL, AN ADVANCEMENT FOR HER.
THE PARENTS WERE SO GRATEFUL THAT I
TOOK THE RISK GIVING THEIR DAUGHTER
SUCH A BREAK THAT LED TO A FULLER LIFE.

2 Corinthians 5:16 "So stop evaluating Christians by what the world thinks about them or by what they seem to be like on the outside . . . Once I thought of Christ that way, merely as a human being like myself: how different I feel now."

ON THE NINTH DAY OF CHRISTMAS

I WAS INTERVIEWING A STUDENT APPLICANT
FOR A TEMPORARY SUMMER JOB.
I CAME ACROSS A YOUNG HIGH SCHOOL STUDENT
LIVING IN A HALFWAY HOUSE FOR
DRUG AND SUBSTANCE ABUSE IN PARK RIDGE, IL, U.S.A.

WITHOUT A DOUBT I DECIDED TO GIVE THIS YOUNG MAN
AN OPPORTUNITY TO START A NEW LIFE
SO HE BACAME A PART OF OUR WORK TEAM.
ONE EARLY MORNING I RECEIVED A CALL
FROM HIS DAD WHO COULDN'T CONTAIN HIS
APPRECIATION AND GRATITUDE
THAT HIS SON WAS GIVEN A NEW HOPE
THAT MIGHT LEAD HIM OUT OF THE HALFWAY HOUSE
BACK TO HIS LOVING PARENTS.

Hebrews 13:2 "Don't forget to be kind to strangers, for some who have done this have entertained angels without realizing it."

ON THE TENTH DAY OF CHRISTMAS

HERE IN CHICAGO, IL, U.S.A. OUR
DOORBELL RANG. I LOOKED THROUGH
THE GLASS OF THE ENTRANCE DOOR
AND SAW A HANDICAPPED-LOOKING
YOUNG MAN I'VE NEVER SEEN BEFORE.

I OPENED THE DOOR, LET HIM IN
AND ASKED WHAT I CAN DO FOR HIM.
HIS CAR HAD A FLAT TIRE FEW HOUSES
DOWN THE ROAD FROM OUR HOUSE.
HE NEEDED TO CALL HIS MOM HOME
FOR HELP.

I ASKED HIM TO HAVE A SEAT,
GAVE HIM OUR CORDLESS PHONE
AND OFFERED HIM SOMETHING
TO QUENCHED HIS THIRST.
HE TALKED TO HIS MOM,
WE CHATTED FOR A WHILE,
THEN HE SAID HIS MOM'S COMING.
HE THEN THANKED ME
FOR LETTING HIM IN AND USE OUR PHONE.

Matthew 25:45 "And I will answer 'when you refused to help the least of these my brothers, you were refusing help to me'."

ON THE ELEVENTH DAY OF CHRISTMAS

IT WAS ADVENT SEASON. PASTOR JUDITH KELSEY-POWELL,
OUR UNITED CHURCH OF THE MEDICAL CENTER,
CHICAGO, IL PASTOR CALLED UP, SHARED
A STORY OF ONE OF HER HIV/AIDS
POSITIVE DYING PATIENT'S CHRISTMAS WISH.
TO HAVE A CHRISTMAS TREE THIS CHRISTMAS
AT LEAST BEFORE HE DIED.
THE FAMILY LIVE IN A TRAILER HOUSE.
PASTOR JUDITH ASKED ME IF I COULD
HELP HER MAKE THIS YOUNG
DYING MAN'S WISH A REALITY.

SHE ASKED IF I COULD DONATE A CHRISTMAS TREE.
WITHOUT A THOUGHT I ASKED HER TO
COME TO MY APARTMENT.
I GAVE MY CHRISTMAS TREE TO FULFILL
THIS YOUNG MAN'S WISH.

WEEKS AFTER CHRISTMAS PASTOR JUDITH
CALLED UP AGAIN, THIS TIME TO LET ME KNOW
HER PATIENT PASSED AWAY.
BUT BEFORE PASSING AWAY, HE WAS THANKFUL
AND HAPPY THAT FINALLY THEY HAD A
CHRISTMAS TREE IN THEIR TRAILER HOUSE.

RESPECTING THIS TRAGIC LIFE STORY,
FOR YEARS I DIDN'T PUT UP CHRISTMAS TREE
ANYMORE AT HOME. IT WAS JUST TWO YEARS
AGO THAT I STARTED PUTTING UP A MINI FIBER OPTIC
CHRISTMAS TREE, NOT LIKE THE ONE I GAVE AWAY.

Hebrews 13:16 "Don't forget to do good and to share what you have with those in need, for such sacrifices are very pleasing to him."

ON THE TWELFTH DAY OF CHRISTMAS

OUR UNITED METHODIST CHURCH,
NORTHERN ILLINOIS CONFERENCE TREASURER
PONG JAVIER CALLED ME AT WORK, 'HI LINDA,
I KNOW THIS IS A LAST MINUTE REQUEST AND NOTICE.
A FAMILY FROM ANGUILA IS COMING
TO OUR CONFERENCE.
THEIR SIX MONTHS OLD BABY NEEDS
MEDICAL SERVICES AT THE SHRINERS HOSPITAL
FOR CHILDREN.

OUR LOCAL COSMOPOLITAN UNITED CHURCH
WAS REQUESTED TO TAKE THIS FAMILY.
OUR PROBLEM IS HOUSING FOR THIS FAMILY
WHILE THEIR BABY IS BEING TREATED.
THEY'RE ARRIVING TOMORROW,
JANUARY 3RD. COULD YOU TAKE THEM IN
YOUR HOUSE?'

WITHOUT A SECOND THOUGHT I SAID 'YES',
I'VE ROOM DOWNSTAIRS IN THE BASEMENT.
AND SO THE FAMILY STAYED WITH US
FOR FULL TWO WEEKS.
OUR PASTOR SCOTT SHREVE,
AND HIS WIFE MARJORIE OFFERED THEM
TRANSPORTATION DURING THE SHUTTLING
BETWEEN SHRINERS HSOPITAL,
CHICAGO CHILDREN'S HOSPITAL,
OUR HOUSE, TO THE GROCERIES
AND THE CHURCH.

WHEN THEY WERE LEAVING GOING BACK TO ANGUILA
THEY COULDN'T CONTAIN THEIR GRATITUDE
FOR BEING UNITED METHODIST CHRISTIANS
GIVEN THIS WARM WELCOME
AND ACCOMODATIONS THRU THE
CHURCHCONNECTION.

***I SHARE THESE OPPORTUNITES WHICH I'VE ENTITLED "THE TWELVE DAYS OF CHRISTMAS ", THOUGH THESE HAPPENED ON DIFFERENT TIMES DURING MY JOURNEY, NOT NECESSARILY ON THE TWELVE DAYS OF CHRISTMAS. I ENTITLED IT SO AS I REFLECT EVERY CHRISTMAS DAY CELEBRATION I HAVE HAD THESE OPPORTUNITIES IN LIFE OF SHARING, GIVING, SACRIFICING AND CARING FOR OTHERS. THAT CHRISTMAS IS NOT JUST ONCE A YEAR ON CHRISTMAS DAY CELEBRATION AND GIFT-GIVING BUT IS AN ALL-YEAR SHARING OF LOVE AND COMPASSION TO THOSE IN NEED AROUND US!

WE DO NOT NEED TO WAIT EVERY CHRISTMAS DAY TO DO GOOD, SHARE GIFTS OF LOVE, CARE AND COMPASSION TO OTHERS. EVERY MINUTE IS AN OPPORTUNITY FOR US IF WE LOOK AROUND AND IS WILLING TO CELEBRATE THE MEANING OF CHRISTMAS IN OUR LIVES! AFTER ALL, WE DO SAY, "IT IS BETTER TO GIVE THAN TO RECEIVE . . ." SO LET US PUT SOME ACTIONS INTO THESE WORDS! OUR DAILY ARMOUR TO CARRY WITH US IS 1 CORINTHIANS 13:13 THERE ARE THREE THINGS THAT REMAIN—FAITH, HOPE, AND LOVE—AND THE GREATEST OF THESE IS LOVE."

As I write this poem the war in Iraq is still the headlines of news media, and great debates in Washington, DC. Having been through World War II and the Vietnam War I couldn't avoid but recollect my participation in a United Methodist Northern Illinois Conference Program entitled "Teaching Toward a Faithful Vision Shalom", by the task force on Christian education for world peace. 1977.

WEAPONS INTO PLOWSHARES

A WISHFUL THINKING CAN BECOME A DREAM
A REALITY IF WE ALL TOGETHER RALLY BEHIND
WEAPONS INTO PLOWSHARES OUR COMMON GOAL.

TRUTH OF THE MATTER WE ALL LOVE LIFE,
LIFE WITHOUT FEAR, YET FULL OF TRUST
SHOULDER TO SHOULDER, HAND IN HAND.
IN OUR JOURNEY WALKING UP AND DOWN
THROUGH VALLEYS AND MEADOWS.
BLISSFULL MOUNTAINTOPS!

FRIENDLY ENVIRONMENT, NO SOUND OF BOMBS
DROPPING EVERYWHERE, AROUND THE GLOBE.
NO SIGHT OF GUNS WIELD BY PEOPLE
AGAINST OTHERS IN SIGHT AIMED TO SHOOT.

ALAS IF THOSE WEAPONS OF WAR AND MURDERS
COULD JUST BE TURNED INTO PLOWSHARES
WHAT A HAVEN OF PEACEFUL LIVING TO SHARE!
BARREN LANDS TILLED TO BE FERTILE
WITH THESE PLOWSHARES TO FEED THE WORLDS'
HUNGRY MEMBERS OF THE HUMAN FAMILY!

Once I overheard a person say . . . "There will never be peace in the Middle East . . ." What a tragic understatement! Yet pages of historical news reveals chaos, crimes and violence in this region for decades to the present!

UNITY AMIDST DIVERSITY

IMAGINE AN ORCHESTRA BAND
PLAYING SO HARMONIOUSLY
AMIDST DIVERSITY OF INSTRUMENTS
EACH MEMBER PLAYING.
WHAT A BEAUTIFUL MELODY OF MUSIC
THE BAND PRODUCES,
WITH EACH INSTRUMENT SO DIFFERENT FROM EACH OTHER.
NOT ONLY INSTRUMENT DIVERSITY BUT, MOST,
IS HUMAN DIVERSITY IN CULTURE, ROOTS, RACE, ORIGIN

NOW CLOSE YOUR EYES AND VISUALIZE A GLOBAL,
HUMAN FAMILY AS DIVERSIFIED AS THE MUSICAL
INSTRUMENTS IN AN ORCHESTRA BAND LIVING IN PEACE,
AND HARMONY WITH ONE ANOTHER, WHAT A GRACE
AND GLORY FOR EVERYONE ON THIS PLANET EARTH!
TO FULFILL A WORLD WIDE DREAM OF PEACE!

A CHALLENGE TO ALL TO DROP ARMS INTO PLOWSHARES
RESPECT EACH CULTURAL ETHNICITY, RELIGION, RACES.
RENDER EACH DUE DIGNITY AMIDST DIVERSITY
TEAR DOWN BARRIERS, IMAGINARY BOUNDARIES.
BE MINDFULL AND SENSITIVE AS WE LIVE TOGETHER
GUARDING EACH OTHER'S PRIVACY, AND BECOME BETTER.

WON'T WE BE THAT ORCHESTRA BAND
PLAYING HARMONIOUSLY,
LIVING TOGETHER ON THIS MOTHER EARTH
IN PEACE AND HARMONY?
THINK ABOUT IT, IS THIS HUMANLY POSSIBLE? I BELIEVE IT IS
ONLY IF WE SEEK THE TRUTH THAT
SHALL MAKE US ALL FREE.
FREE OF HARM, HATRED, BITTERNESS, ENVY AND GREED.
INSTEAD WEARING THE ARMOUR OF LOVE AND
FORGIVENESS.

As I go through the Old Testament book of Genesis, the story of Abraham and Sarah / Sarai; the story of Hagar, the slave girl; the birth of Isaac and the birth of Ishmael. I was challenged to create this poem:

ONE BODY A UNIVERSAL FAMILY

THE CREATION STORY, THE GARDEN OF EDEN
THE HOUSEHOLD OF ABRAHAM, ALL THESE
BRING ONE MESSAGE,
WE ALL CAME FROM THE SAME HUMAN FAMILY
ADOPTED VARIED LAND AND CULTURE
COVERING THE EARTH WITH VARIETY OF COLORS,
INTER ETHNICAL, MULTI-RELIGIOSITY.

WHAT A GIFT GIVEN TO US TO RESPECT AND VALUE
TO LIVE SIDE BY SIDE, LIKE THE LAMB AND THE LION.
TO LOVE AND FORGIVE AS THE NEED ARISE.
NEEDLESS TO SAY PEACEFUL CO-EXISTENCE,
NOT INDEPENDENCE RATHER INTERDEPENDENCE.

NO MAN IS AN ISLAND SO THE CLICHÉ SAYS
WE ALL NEED EACH OTHER TO CARE FOR AND PROTECT,
NOT TO DESTROY A RACE BUT TO KEEP EACH IDENTITY.
THAT WE ALL ENJOY THE BEAUTY OF THE EARTH
BEING ONE FAMILY WITH GREAT DIGNITY.